MW01254610

A Keepsake

BRANDYWINE VALLEY

Antelo Devereux Jr.

4880 Lower Valley Road • Atglen, PA 19310

INTRODUCTION

The Brandywine Valley has become a brand name for a historic and picturesque region outside Philadelphia that approximately corresponds to the watershed of Brandywine Creek. The photographs roughly follow the creek from its headwaters in the Welsh Mountains of Chester County, Pennsylvania, to Chadds Ford, and the historic mill areas outside Wilmington, Delaware.

More than 300 years have passed since Chester County, along with Philadelphia and Bucks Counties, was organized by William Penn, whose father received a large land grant from English King Charles II in 1681. The grant included all lands north to south between the 40th and 43rd parallels and the Delaware and Susquehanna Rivers east to west. Indigenous Native American inhabitants—the Lenni-Lenape and Susquehanna cultures—were succeeded by colonial settlers: primarily English, Welsh, and German Protestants, Quakers, and Amish.

Philadelphia was the birth place of the United States, and Chester County, to the southwest, provided the natural resources that helped support the nation-to-be. The county's fertile land produced an abundance of food. Its streams, such as Brandywine Creek, provided energy for mills, while forgings from rudimentary iron mines and furnaces were used for war and peace. Agriculture remains a key part of the county's economy, which is now diverse and fully part of the twenty-first century. The digital age lives alongside the Amish.

Thanks to determined and successful efforts by the Brandywine Conservancy and similar organizations to save the area from development and maintain open space, a significant amount of land is under easement and remains undeveloped. Considering its close proximity to Philadelphia, Chester County and the Brandywine Valley form a very desirable place to live, work, and visit.

I hope the following images will give the viewer a sense of the beauty, history, and life of the Brandywine Valley and its environs. It has been a fun challenge capturing and editing them for this book. No doubt many wonderful places and buildings have been omitted, but such is the difficult process of editing.

Honey Brook

Honey Brook

Honey Brook

Honey Brook

Honey Brook

West Nantmeal

Fallowfield

Isabella Forge (private), West Nantmeal

West Nantmeal

West Nantmeal

Marsh Creek State Park, Upper Uwchlan

West Brandywine

Springton Manor, Wallace

Hibernia Mansion, West Caln

Old Fiddlers' Picnic, Hibernia County Park

Coatesville

West Chester

West Chester

West Chester University, West Chester

West Chester

East Bradford

Marshallton

Ercildoun

West Marlborough

Downingtown

Brandywine River

Great Blue Heron

Canada Geese

London Grove Township

New Garden Airport

Brandywine Creek

New Garden Airport

Creamery, Kennett Square

West Marlborough

West Marlborough

London Grove

London Grove

Radnor Races in support of the Brandywine Conservancy

London Grove

West Marlborough

Newlin

Anselma Mill, West Pikeland

HERE RESTS
INDIAN HANNAH
THE LAST OF THE LENNI-LENAPE
INDIANS IN CHESTER COUNTY
WHO DIED IN 1802

MARKED BY
CHESTER COUNTY HISTORICAL SOCIETY
1909

Kennett

The Laurels, East Fallowfield

The Laurels, East Fallowfield

The Laurels, East Fallowfield

Doe Run, West Marlborough

Brandywine Creek, Newlin

West Marlborough

West Marlborough

Penn Oak, London Grove Meeting

Stroud Water Reseach Center — "We Grow Trees for Clean Water," Avondale

Galer Estate Winery, East Marlborough

Fusell Farm, Kennett—underground railroad site

Kennett Square

Kennett Square

Kennett Square

Phillips Mushrooms, Kennett Square

Farmers market, Kennett Square

Cinco de Mayo, Kennett Square

Primitive Hall, West Marlborough

Dilworthtown

Longwood Gardens

Longwood Gardens

Longwood Gardens

Longwood Gardens

Longwood Gardens

William Brinton House, 1704, Birmingham

Birmingham Lafayette Cemetery, Birmingham

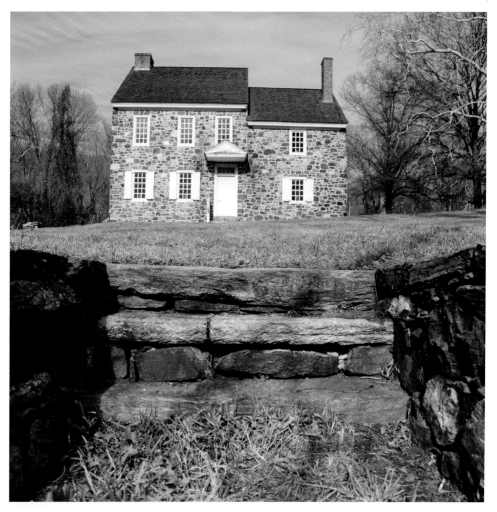

Washington's Headquarters, Chadds Ford

Brandywine Battlefied, Chadds Ford

John Chad's House, Chadds Ford

Gilpin Farm, Brandywine Battlefield, Chadds Ford

Brandywine River Museum of Art, Chadds Ford

Brandywine River Museum of Art, Chadds Ford

Kuerner's Hill, Chadds Ford

Chadds Ford

Kuerner's Barn, Chadds Ford

N. C. Wyeth studio, Chadds Ford

Winterthur House and Museum, Greenville, Delaware

Hagley Museum, Montchanin, Delaware

Hagley Museum, Montchanin, Delaware

Hagley Museum, Montchanin, Delaware

Antelo Devereux Jr. has been photographing for the better part of his life, first as an amateur and more recently as a professional. He has published seven books and has exhibited his images in various venues and galleries in Maine, Vermont, Pennsylvania, and Delaware. He has degrees from Harvard University and the University of Pennsylvania and has studied at Maine Media Workshops. He lives with his family in Pennsylvania and summers in Maine. His photographs can be seen on Instagram.
@photoeye1

Designed by Molly Shields
Type set in Bell MT

ISBN: 978-0-7643-5574-5
Printed in China

Published by Schiffer Publishing, Ltd.
4880 Lower Valley Road
Atglen, PA 19310
Phone: (610) 593-1777; Fax: (610) 593-2002
E-mail: Info@schifferbooks.com
Web: www.schifferbooks.com

For our complete selection of fine books on this and related subjects, please visit our website at www.schifferbooks.com. You may also write for a free catalog.

Schiffer Publishing's titles are available at special discounts for bulk purchases for sales promotions or premiums. Special editions, including personalized covers, corporate imprints, and excerpts, can be created in large quantities for special needs. For more information, contact the publisher.

We are always looking for people to write books on new and related subjects. If you have an idea for a book, pleas contact us at proposals@schifferbooks.com.

Antelo Devereux Jr. has been photographing for the better part of his life, first as an amateur and more recently as a professional. He has published seven books and has exhibited his images in various venues and galleries in Maine, Vermont, Pennsylvania, and Delaware. He has degrees from Harvard University and the University of Pennsylvania and has studied at Maine Media Workshops. He lives with his family in Pennsylvania and summers in Maine. His photographs can be seen on Instagram.

@photoeye1

Designed by Molly Shields
Type set in Bell MT

ISBN: 978-0-7643-5574-5
Printed in China

Published by Schiffer Publishing, Ltd.
4880 Lower Valley Road
Atglen, PA 19310
Phone: (610) 593-1777; Fax: (610) 593-2002
E-mail: Info@schifferbooks.com
Web: www.schifferbooks.com

For our complete selection of fine books on this and related subjects, please visit our website at www.schifferbooks.com. You may also write for a free catalog.

Schiffer Publishing's titles are available at special discounts for bulk purchases for sales promotions or premiums. Special editions, including personalized covers, corporate imprints, and excerpts, can be created in large quantities for special needs. For more information, contact the publisher.

We are always looking for people to write books on new and related subjects. If you have an idea for a book, please contact us at proposals@schifferbooks.com.